The PEACE *of* GOD

A Key to discovering the Secrets of Faith

NANASEI OPOKU-SARKODIE

Unless otherwise indicated, all scripture quotations are taken from the King James Version, Amplified Bible, New English Translation, New international Version of the Holy Bible.

THE PEACE OF GOD
ISBN: 978-9988-2-9415-1
Copyright c2019 by REVEREND NANASEI OPOKU-SARKODIE

Published by
Paradise Publication

For your personal copy of this, information about other books by the author or bulk purchase please contact +233 (0)242472655/ (0)505286112 / (0) 274009933

TABLE OF CONTENTS

- What is the peace of God?

- If you want to walk in the Peace of God, avoid sin.

- The Peace of God is a weapon.

- Maintaining Peace during warfare.

- Your Peace is a proof of your victory.

- Whenever you don't have peace, you have war.

- The Peace of God makes you keep trying even when you are losing.

PREFACE

Jesus said in John 14:27,

"Peace I leave you, my peace I give you: not as the world gives, give I unto you. Let not your heart be troubled, neither let it be afraid".

Which means that, the world can give you a form of peace, but it cannot be compared to the one Jesus left for us. The peace of God is so crucial that when Jesus was leaving, He didn't leave His disciples anything but His peace.

The Peace of God is a weapon that calms every reaction in times of trouble. When Jesus and His disciples encountered a storm in the boat, the only weapon that could calm that reaction was the weapon of peace; "Peace be still". When the Israelites got to the red sea and thought all hope was lost, they started complaining to Moses, but watch what Moses told them, ***"Fear not, stand still, and see the salvation of the Lord; which he will show you today: for the Egyptians whom you have seen today, you shall see them again no more forever. The Lord shall fight for you and you shall hold your Peace." (Ex. 14:13-14).***

God is saying that anytime you are confronted with a situation, Standstill. It means that you must first establish the peace of God.

The source of the Peace of God is God Himself. So, anytime you are connected to the Peace of God, you are connected to God Himself. For you to establish the Peace of God, you must first have a relationship with His son, Jesus Christ, because God doesn't know anyone who has not made Jesus Christ Lord of his or her life. When you establish the Peace of

God, you naturally establish peace with yourself and peace with others.

When we abide in the Peace of God, it becomes a fortress and a weapon the devil cannot stand. Anytime we establish the Peace of God, it is a major blow against the devil and against his two trusted weapons - fear and oppression. That was why the devil couldn't understand it when Jesus slept on that stormy boat. Jesus was at rest because He had already seen Himself on the other side. I strongly believe that by the time you finish reading this book, you will sleep over that marital storm, you will sleep over that financial storm and you will sleep over any other storm you may encounter in life because your faith will be rekindled. May the Lord watch over you and keep you.

CHAPTER ONE
THE PEACE OF GOD

- What is the peace of God?

- If you want to walk in the peace of God, avoid sin.

- The peace of God is a weapon.

- Maintaining peace during warfare.

WHAT IS THE PEACE OF GOD?

The Peace of God is the state of calmness or quietness of the spirit that transcends or surpasses every circumstance in life.

Philippians 4:7 says "...the Peace of God surpasses all understanding...". This is a supernatural peace that comes from God during our times of struggle. It is beyond all human understanding. - *And the peace of God, which surpasses all understanding, will guard your hearts and minds through Jesus Christ (Philippians 4:7).*

Because we have trusted Jesus Christ as our Savior, we can experience this wonderful peace of God no matter what the circumstances. This is a peace that unbelievers cannot understand or experience.

The term Peace is described in scripture as a gift from God which corresponds with His nature - "The God of Peace" - 1 Thess 5:23, Heb 13:20.

"And the very God of peace sanctify you wholly; and I pray God your whole spirit and soul and body be preserved blameless unto the coming of our Lord Jesus Christ". 1 Thess 5:23

"Now the God of peace, that brought again from the dead our Lord Jesus, that great shepherd of the sheep, through the blood of the everlasting covenant". Hebrews 13:20

The source of this Peace is God himself because He is called the God of peace. If God is Peace, then all you need to do to experience His Peace is to draw closer to Him. The more we draw closer to Him, the more we can enjoy His Peace.

Living in the Peace of God can be compared to the petals of a flower unfolding in the morning sunlight. The petals of Peace in our lives unfolds as we learn more about God. We will discover that He is a faithful God and His goodness and mercies endures forever. We refuse to allow certain circumstances in life to determine our level of contentment. Rather, we will choose to rely upon the character of God which never changes (The Peace of God). When we develop a lifestyle of making the Lord our refuge, we will forever abide in His Peace.

…If you want to walk in the Peace of God, avoid Sin

If you want to walk in the Peace of God, get to know Jesus as your Lord and personal Saviour and try as much as possible to avoid sin.

Do you know that you cannot have the peace of God until you are first at peace with God? Until we are brought to repentance and faith, we are enemies of God. *For if, when we were enemies, we were reconciled to God by the death of his Son, much more, being reconciled, we shall be saved by his life. (Rom 5:10).* Our natural minds cannot even understand the things of God. *"Because the carnal mind is enmity against God: for it is not subject to the law of God, neither indeed can be." (Rom 8:7).* This is why God has to quicken us or make us alive in Christ because we were dead in our sins *(Eph 2:1),* and you know that people who are dead cannot even know God in a personal way. It took the power and the love of God to make us new creations in Christ (2Cor 5:17). So that we will be able to accept His Word and by extension, His Peace. So, until we are at peace with God, we can never have the peace of God. The Apostle Paul wrote, ***"Since we have been justified by faith, we have peace with God through our Lord Jesus Christ" (Rom 5:1)***, and this is the kind of peace which surpasses all understanding.

Whenever you are dealing with the devil, make sure you are not living in sin which is also carnality. One of the most powerful statements Jesus made before His crucifixion was this, ***"...for the ruler of this world is coming, and he has nothing in Me" (John 14:30).*** This means that the devil can have his ammunition in you. If you are fornicating, he has an ammunition in you; if you are a gossip, he has an ammunition in you; if you are a thief, he has an ammunition in you.

To truly walk in the peace of God, you must first avoid sin. If you are living in sin, you cannot establish the peace of God. Anytime you deny your old life and pick up the new life, you have established the Peace of God. That is why the Bible says, ***"If a man is in Christ, he is a new creation, old things are passed away; behold, all things have become new" (2 Cor. 5:17).***

…The Peace of God is a weapon

"And the God of Peace will soon crush satan under your feet …" (Romans 16:20 NIV)

Whenever we maintain Peace during warfare, it is a major blow against the devil and against his two powerful weapons (fear and oppression). The devil is such that you cannot stop him from attacking you. If he stops attacking you, it means that he has been fired from his job. It is the devil's responsibility to attack you but it is your responsibility not to allow him to prevail over you.

The fact that the devil is attacking you does not mean that he must automatically prevail over you. This is the scripture, *"No weapon formed against you shall prosper…" (Isa. 54:17):-* you cannot stop his weapons from forming, but you must make sure he doesn't prosper. If the devil doesn't attack you, how will you see the manifestation of God's power in your life? Without Pharaoh's attack on the Israelites, we wouldn't have had the recorded miracles in Egypt. Without Goliath, nobody would have heard of David. So, your attack is a contact for your promotion and it is also a contact for God's name to be glorified.

God is saying in the above scripture that, He has a weapon that can crush the devil, and this weapon is not fasting and prayer, but His Peace. Some weapons can push the devil; but even when you push something, that thing stands a chance of coming back. All the blood can do is to overcome but Peace crushes.

"The God of peace will soon crush Satan under your feet. The grace of our Lord Jesus be with you. Amen".(Rom 16:20).

Whenever you crush something, you establish permanent dominion over that thing and render it powerless and impotent.

The Peace of God is a weapon, and the purpose of this weapon is to give God the opportunity to fight for you. The reason your battle is so fierce and so intimidating is that you have not given God the opportunity to fight for you. Sometimes, we act as if we can fight the battle ourselves. To establish spiritual authority and position yourself in a way for God to fight for you, you need to maintain the Peace of God. The reason is that; when it comes to spiritual battles, only God can fight. You can pray but you cannot kill a demon.

"And he arose, and rebuked the wind and said unto the sea, Peace, be still. And the wind ceased, and there was a great calm"-Mark 4:39

Peace is a weapon that has the power to silence every storm in your life; be it a marital storm or a financial storm. In the battle of life, your Peace is actually your weapon. Someone was sleeping in a storm, woke up, and rebuked the storm and said, "Be still". Which means that you must rest before you rule. If you don't rest, you can never rule. In the next chapter, I will be dealing with the subject: **Rest before you rule.** The reason Jesus ruled over that storm was that he was resting. Do you want to rule over hardship? Then rest. Another word for 'Rest' here is 'Peace'. The twelve disciples that were not resting couldn't rule, but the one that rested ruled.

A lot of people are not ruling over their matrimonial homes because they are not resting. Only the Peace of God can calm every reaction in times of trouble. The reason is that the source of this Peace, is God Himself. So, whenever you are connected to the Peace of God, you are connected to God Himself.

... Maintaining Peace during warfare

Study most great men of God; they fight battles with Peace because it is dangerous to reply to criticisms. The Bible says, *"Even a fool, when he holds his peace, is counted wise...." (Prov. 17:28).* Imagine someone was provoking you, and everybody was expecting you to react but you were laughing; people will even think that you are not a human being because we live in times that people find it very difficult to tolerate certain things in life. Only the peace of God can let you handle certain difficult issues with ease.

Anytime you don't have control over a situation, establish the Peace of God over that situation. One day, a lady came to me and said, her husband was cheating on her. You could actually see that she was growing lean. I looked at her and told her, "Girl, I promise you one thing, you are going to die and when you die, your husband will attend your funeral with his new girlfriend." You are growing lean over an adulterous man who is growing fat. And I asked her, "Since you began to worry, has it changed anything?" And she said, "No". Then I said to her, "You are trying to fight a battle you have no power to fight." She asked me, "Daddy, what should I do?" I said to her, "Establish the Peace of God."

Let me tell you one thing, the peace of God doesn't just come; you need the grace to practice it because of the depth of worries you have planted yourself into. Sometimes, I see pastors walking around looking very depressed; perhaps, they are thinking of how to build a small auditorium and they don't know how. When we started building Potter's City, I was looking very lean. I grew lean to the point that one of my daughters in the church saw me one day and started crying. I even taught something was wrong with her. She got so worried but her worries couldn't change anything. I also discovered that anytime I got worried, projects in Potter's City starts slowing down.

Everything in the atmosphere is trying to steal your Peace. The devil's number one attack is to steal your Peace. You cannot sing, you cannot dance, and you cannot laugh, because you have lost your Peace. This Peace of God I am talking about is not the absence of troubles in your life, but rejoicing in the midst of all the troubles because you know your Redeemer lives. This is what Moses told the Israelites,

"Fear not, stand still, and see the salvation of the Lord, which he will show you today: for the Egyptians whom you have seen today, you shall

see them again no more forever. The Lord shall fight for you, and you shall hold your Peace" (Ex. 14:13-14).

The Lord is saying here that before you fight the battle, 'Standstill'. It means that you must first establish the Peace of God.

CHAPTER TWO

REST BEFORE YOU RULE

- Your peace is a proof of your victory.

- Whenever you don't have peace, you have war.

- The peace of God makes you keep trying even when you are losing.

"Now when Jesus saw great multitudes about him, he gave commandment to depart unto the other side…. And when he was entered into a ship, his disciples followed him. And behold, there arose a great tempest in the sea, in so much that the ship was covered with the waves: but he was asleep" - Matthew 8:18; 23-24

How do you sleep in a boat that is about to capsize? How do you sleep in an economy that is failing? Some of Jesus' disciples were actually generational fishermen; and for that storm to threaten them, then it must have been a terrible one. But how on earth do you sleep in such a terrible storm? I know the marriage is threatening you, I know the business is threatening you, I know your bank account is threatening you, but go and sleep.

Do you know why when there is an accident, babies don't die? Because they don't come under any apprehension and fear. Most of the things that kill you are as a result of fear and apprehension. Fear and faith operate with the same principle. Faith is the practical expression of confidence in God and His word. Fear is the practical expression of confidence in the devil and his word. So, what you hear either brings fear or faith.

To establish the Peace of God, control your eye gate and your ear gate. Be careful what you hear with your ears and what you see with your eyes.

The Bible says the man, Jesus, who had established the Peace of God was sleeping in the storm. So, one of the signs that shows that you have established the Peace of God is when even in the midst of crisis, even in the midst of oppositions, even in the midst of difficulties, you are resting because you know your Redeemer lives. Jesus didn't say, ***"Let us go and drown". He said, "Let us go to the other side".*** The disciples who had not established the Peace of God saw it as a storm that drowns but the man, Jesus, who had established the Peace of God saw it as a good time for resting.

When you go to the office and they tell you that they are going to lay off workers, remember this key **(The Peace of God).** Assuming they even succeed in laying off workers, if you establish the Peace of God, you will get a better job than those who have not established the Peace of God. You worry so much about things you don't have control over. What have all the apprehensions, the anxieties, and the sleepless nights added to the situation? People are now growing faster than their ages because they have not established the Peace of God. If the man we are all following slept on a stormy boat, then you should be able to sleep in that marital trouble, you should able to sleep with a doctor's report; because there is a God in heaven. Let me tell you one thing; if you establish the Peace of God and get a breakthrough, God will still be God. If you decide to walk in your anxiety, there is nothing that will change God to be a man. So, you better go by the way He is teaching you, for Him to visit you.

...Your Peace is a proof of your victory

Your Peace is an authentic proof of your uncompromising victory. If you allow the Peace of God to go, satan has stolen your victory. Jesus gave a reply to His disciples and said, ***"Why are you fearful, o you of little faith?" (Matt. 8:26).*** Why are you having sleepless nights? People are sitting in the church full of fear; fear of tomorrow, fear of not getting married, fear of "I may not have a child", fear of traveling. "O you of little faith". Anytime you don't have Peace, your faith is little. If you lose the Peace of God, your faith becomes impotent.

Jesus got up and rebuked the wind and it became completely calm. ***"But the men marveled, saying, what manner of man is this, that even the winds and the sea obey him" (Matt 8:27).*** When you establish the Peace of God, people will begin asking, what kind of man is this? What kind of woman is this? It is only when you begin to walk in the Peace of God that people ask these questions.

One of the trusted plans of the devil is to rob us of our Peace. If he succeeds in robbing us of our Peace, the rest of the weapons don't matter to him anymore. Satan fears virtue, and Peace is a virtue. I am not saying that attacks won't come your way, I am also not saying that you are going to get everything on a silver platter. All I am saying is that in the midst of the storm, establish the Peace of God. God will visit you in that situation because the Peace of God attracts supernatural attention.

...Whenever you don't have Peace, you have war

Anytime you don't establish the Peace of God, in the realms of the spirit, you are at war; and how long will you continue to be at war? Don't try to fight battles only God can fight. The Israelites complained to Moses, ***"We could have died in Egypt; look at them coming"***. Moses said to the people, ***"Fear not, standstill and see the salvation of the Lord, which he will show to you today: for the Egyptians whom you have seen today, you shall see them again no more forever. The Lord shall fight for you, and you shall hold your Peace. (Ex. 14:12-14).*** Establish the Peace of God and see the deliverance of the Lord, establish the Peace of God and see the healing of the Lord.

Whenever you have Peace, war runs away. The Peace of God attracts joy, the

Peace of God attracts self-control, the Peace of God attracts goodness, and the Peace of God attracts gentleness. ***"Blessed are the Peacemakers: for they shall be called the children of God" (Matt 5:9).*** So, if you have not established the Peace of God, you are not a child of God. Anytime satan steals your Peace, you automatically become like him.

The lack of this Peace has caused people to even marry their businesses. They work so much that they don't even have time to enjoy the fruit of their labor. The devil is such that he can program you to overwork yourself.

Lack of this Peace can lead you to make stupid decisions and regret later in the future because when you lack Peace, you lack patience. When you see someone who has lost his patience, it means that he has lost his Peace, because

Peace naturally gives you patience. The peace of God frees you from any anxiety, it frees you from apprehension, and it frees you from stress.

...The peace of God makes you keep trying even when you are losing

In 1816, his family was forced out of their home and he had to work to support his family. In 1818, his mother died. In 1831, he failed in business. In 1832, he ran for state legislature and lost. In 1832, he also lost his job. In 1833, he borrowed money from a friend to begin a business and by the end of the year, he was bankrupt. He spent the next seventeen years of his life paying for the dept.

In 1834, he ran for state legislature again and won. In 1835 he was engaged to be married but his sweetheart died. In 1836, he had a total nervous breakdown and was in bed for six months. In 1838, he sought to become a speaker of the state legislature and was defeated. In 1843, he ran for Congress and lost. In

1846, he ran for Congress again and this time, he won into Washington and did some good works.

In 1848, he ran for re-election for Congress; even though with all his good works, he still lost. In 1849, he sought for a job of land officer in his home state and was rejected. In 1854, he ran for Senate of the United States and lost. In 1856, he sought for the vice presidential nomination at his party national convention and lost with only a hundred votes. In 1858, he ran for U.S Senate again and lost. In 1860, he was elected as U.S President - Abraham Lincoln.

You need to have the Peace of God to keep trying even when you are losing. There are people whose lives come to an end even when they fail at their first attempt. One thing you must know about the devil is that he doesn't attack anything that doesn't have a future.

Never give up! Don't lose your Peace and be in so much want because when you are in a hurry, you will die in worries. You cannot say that because you failed in that examination, your life is over. One day, my Mathematics teacher entered the classroom with a cutlass, and when he entered, everybody started running. Then he shouted, "Stay! I brought this to Nanasei". Just because I was not doing well in his subject, he brought me a cutlass to go and weed. I grew up to discover that I was not born a Mathematician but when you give me a microphone, deliverance will come to the oppressed and healing will come to the sick. I found Jesus and He changed my life.

The Peace of God will let you discover the purpose of God for your life. Don't kill yourself because of that examination. Don't lose hope because of that job. Don't let news of the economy bring you down. Establish the Peace of God because *"A man's gift makes room for him…." (Prov. 18:16).*

Remember what God told you in the beginning. When the disciples came under apprehension and fear, thinking they were going to drown, they had forgotten what Jesus told them earlier, "Let us go to the other side". They didn't believe what Jesus said. Jesus didn't say "Let us go and drown". He said, "Let us go to the other side".

What has God said about your life? Anytime God says something and you doubt Him, you make him a liar. His greatest pain is when you doubt Him and His greatest pleasure is when you believe Him. Do you believe the prophecy that says you are going to get a breakthrough? As for God, He has already released the answer. It is your attitude and lack of the peace of God that is delaying the manifestation of your blessings.

One of the major demonstrations of unbelief is to ask God for something He has already given you. For instance, if you are sick, as a child of God, you don't pray for God to heal you. Your healing has already been paid for. So, all you need to do is to appropriate it. ***"But he was wounded for our transgressions, he was bruised for our iniquities; the chastisement of our peace was upon him, and with his stripes, we are healed." (Isaiah 54:5)***

CHAPTER THREE

"LET US GO TO THE OTHER SIDE"

- Ignorance is the strength of the oppressor.

- Rise up! We are going to the other side.

- Leave the battle for God.

...Ignorance is the strength of the oppressor

What you don't know can destroy you. Once you don't know, satan will take advantage over it and destroy you. Do you know why your marriage is in turbulence? Because you had no knowledge of the guy before you married him and vice versa. Jesus didn't say "Let us go and drown". That was why he went to sleep. As far as Jesus was concerned, drowning was not part of the equation.

When God called you, he didn't say sickness was going to kill you. I am very confident about this: if the rapture delays, I will be eighty years and still be preaching like the way I am preaching. I am very sure about this because there is no arrow the devil hasn't shot. It is not the arrow but the one on my side.

David said, ***"When I walk through the valley of the shadows of death, I will fear no evil for you are with me…." (Psalm 23:4).*** What threatens you does not threaten your God. So, make sure you are closer to your God, and let the threat come and meet you with your God. The only problem with you is that when the threat came, you were far from God. Satan cannot deal with you unless he isolates you. Every isolation is a sign of a major satanic attack.

... Rise Up! We are going to the other side

Do you know why you don't have the Peace of God? You have forgotten what God told you in the beginning. We are going to the other side. That is our target; so, anything that happens in between the journey doesn't matter. Our target is to go to the other side. When I prophesied Potter's City many years ago, others got confused and misinterpreted it. I didn't have to let their confusion stop the vision because I was the one who saw it. What have you seen that people are trying to stop it's manifestation?. You have also given them the opportunity to stop it because of your fear and apprehension. You saw your glorious future but along the line, you met someone who messed you up. It doesn't mean that the vision is killed. Rise up! and make sure you get to the other side.

We will surely get to the other side. The economy will not drown us. We don't care who the president becomes, we don't care how much they increase prices of things. As the waters increased, Noah's ark floated above the waters. We may not have the money today but we are excited because we are walking in the Peace of God. If your life is controlled by your bank account, you have missed God.

Do you know why God hasn't blessed you yet? Because he doesn't want to give you money now for the money to have you. The problem is not having the money, the problem is the money having you. That is why a lot of people, when God blesses them a little, they stop coming to church. Abraham's test was not because God wanted to eat Isaac. God wanted to know whether Abraham had Isaac or Isaac had him.

"You shall not make any other God beside me"

Some of you don't have a god as an idol but your boyfriend has become your god, your girlfriend has become your god, your mobile phone has become your god, your business has become your god. Anything that competes with your love for God has become your god. If you marry and your spouse stops you from going to church, he or she has become your idol. What is an idol? An idol is anything that has taken the place of God in your life.

Jesus said, anybody who has not left his or her husband, wife, children, job cannot be His disciple. Jesus is saying that if you want to be His disciple, you must leave those things and follow Him. Which means that, there is a place you come to where you must choose between those things and God. I will advise you to always choose God. My mentor, Papa Oyedepo one day said that his wife was sick and he was going to twenty-one countries preaching the gospel; as a result of that God healed his wife.

...Leave the battle for God

"Unless the Lord builds the house, they labor in vain that builds it. Unless the Lord keeps the city, the watchman wakes, but in vain." - Psalm 127:1

Don't follow Babylon because Babylon is falling. Don't envy their cars and their money because they can't sleep at night. That is why they are always looking stressful. You have a living God but there are rulers of darkness contending with you; so, leave the battle for God. The worries and anxieties of this world are making a lot of people grow even faster than their ages, and the sad thing is that the children of God are now behaving like unbelievers. Instead of the church judging the world, the world is now judging the church. Some of you are only christians in the church. You don't behave like children of God in the office. You talk the way they talk, you behave the way they behave and because of that, you have given them an ammunition to fight you.

I have always been saying that no political party will come to power for my life to change, I would have disgraced my God. A child of God must not connect his or her life to a political party. *"….but the people that do know their God shall be strong…." (Dan 11:32).* The problem with you is that you don't know your God. Some of you are living as if you are not children of faith. You live a life of borrowing; where then is the God that supplies all your needs according to Philippians 4:19?. Establish the Peace of God in your heart and attract the supernatural blessings of God.

Can I announce to you one of the keys you need to operate with, for God to prosper you? Don't be envious of anybody and don't be jealous of anyone. Rejoice with them that rejoice. Anybody that has not established the Peace of God will always talk about other people's blessings because of envy. When people don't establish the Peace of God, nothing good attracts them, and they have a problem with everything. You don't come around a pastor and envy what he or she has because you don't know the whole story. Some of the things you are envying, they got them by favor.

The coat of many colors is not sold in the store; a father has to sew it and give it to you. If you are diligent with God's work, God can touch the heart of others to bless you. The Bible says *"He is a rewarder of them that diligently seek Him" (Heb. 11:6).* Just put this principle in perspective and walk in the way He wants you to walk. You cannot live your life the way you are living now and establish the Peace of God. The Peace of

God doesn't just happen. Every blessing of God is conditional. The Bible says, ***"Jesus loved righteousness and hated iniquity, therefore the Lord anointed Him"***. So, the price for anointing is to depart from iniquity.

CHAPTER FOUR
"MY PEACE I GIVE UNTO YOU"

- Establishing the Peace of God comes as a result of your obedience to God.

- How to have and enjoy the Peace of God.

"Peace I leave with you, my peace I give unto you: not as the world gives, give I unto you. Let not your heart be troubled, neither let it be afraid" - John 14:27 KJV

The world can give you a form of peace but it cannot be compared to what Christ left for us. This Peace of God is so crucial that when Jesus was departing, He didn't leave His disciples money, He didn't leave them cars, He didn't leave them anything but His Peace because when you have Peace, you will naturally have everything.

This is the one that holds silver and gold, this is the one that came to stay on earth for thirty-three years and never lacked anything yet he said, I am not leaving you anything but "My Peace". How powerful it is to have this weapon of Peace. I have come to discover that satan fears it more than fasting. It is the only weapon that crashes satan under your feet -(Rom. 16:20)

When you have peace with God and peace with yourself, you will naturally have peace with others. You cannot have peace with others when you don't have peace with yourself. That is why Jesus never fought anybody on earth. He even prayed for those who crucified Him because He was at peace with Himself. The Peace of God - it will not let you reply to criticisms, it will not let you react. Anybody that has established the

Peace of God sees insult as an opinion. He or she will not walk in an unforgiving life and resentment. What hurts others cannot hurt them because they have established the Peace of God.

...Establishing the Peace of God comes as a result of your obedience to God

Anytime you don't establish the Peace of God, chances are that you are going where God says you shouldn't go. There are people in the church who don't enjoy Peace because they are going where God has not sent them. There is a prophet in the bible called Jonah. The Lord told him to go and preach to the people in Nineveh. Jonah decided to turn to Tarshish; and Tarshish according to geography, is opposite to Nineveh. Jonah went the opposite direction. Many people don't have the peace of God because they are facing the opposite direction. They are going where God has not sent them. They are doing things contrary to what God has told them.

This is where righteousness, purity, holiness and the fear of God are very crucial because these are things that keep you in the state of Peace. When everybody is lying, speak the truth because truth leads to peace. When everybody is fornicating, live a holy life; when everybody is stealing, work with your hands and you will be different from them.

One thing about the devil is that he can let you have a short-term pleasure for a long-term trouble. The Bible says, ***"Moses preferred to suffer affliction with his brothers and sisters than to enjoy pleasure for a season" (Heb. 11:24-25).*** Which means that if the pleasure is not from God, it is only for a season and the consequence will be a long-term one. You cannot do anything against the truth but for the truth. Anytime you go contrary to God's direction, you compromise your own Peace.

....How to have and enjoy the Peace of God

"Nevertheless the foundation of God stands sure, having this seal, The Lord Knows them that are his. And, let everyone that names the name of Christ depart from iniquity" - 2 Timothy 2:19

Receiving Jesus Christ into your life is enough for you to escape hell but to live a victorious life, you must make Him Lord of your life. A lot of people in the church know Christ but Christ is not Lord over their lives. Another word for 'Lord' is 'Ownership'. If you make Jesus Lord of your life, it means that you don't own yourself again. And if you don't own yourself, then you cannot please yourself but to live a life that pleases God.

One of the reasons a lot of people don't have Peace is because Jesus is not Lord of their lives. If Jesus becomes Lord of your life, you must depart from iniquity. This is the only way to have the peace of God. Nobody can have the peace of God if he or she does not have a relationship with Christ. If you don't make Jesus your personal Lord and Saviour, God doesn't know you.

One day, someone came to me and said, I should pray for him. I asked the person, what do you want me to pray about? He said, "Anything". Then I asked him, do you know Jesus Christ? He replied, "Do I need to know Jesus Christ before you pray for me? I showed him from the Bible that every prayer I pray, God will not answer because the prayer of the sinner is an abomination unto God (Prov. 15:8). So, when you don't know Jesus and you start praying, God gets angry because you don't qualify to use the Name of Jesus. The only prayer of a sinner God accepts is the prayer for salvation. It is after this prayer that God will answer any other prayer. The other issue is this: anybody that doesn't know Jesus is full of iniquity. That was why David said, ***"If I regard iniquity in my heart, the Lord will not hear me" (Ps. 66:18).***

The Peace of God is a choice. Nobody can force it on you. You choose to walk in the Peace of God and there are conditions to walk in it; self-cleansing, you are not living a life contrary to God's Word, you are not doing things that displeases God. It doesn't matter what you lose in life, make sure you don't lose the Peace of God. Let it be a permanent virtue in your life no matter the condition. You will be a major threat to the devil. One of the greatest surprises of the devil was to see Jesus sleep in a storm. Nothing harasses the devil than when he shoots his best arrows and applies his best weapons and you are still standing. Sometimes, God waits for the devil to do his worst before He comes in to do His best. So, don't worry about the fact that the situation is getting worse. God is patiently waiting for the devil to do his worse. After that God will ask him, "What else can you do?"

CHAPTER FIVE

ENEMIES OF THE PEACE OF GOD

- Refusing to walk in love.

- Refusing to grow.

- Refusing to walk in humility.

... Refusing to walk in Love

"Though I speak with the tongues of men and of angels, and have no love, I am become as sounding brass, or a clanging cymbal" - 1 Corinthians 13:1 KJV

"And though I have the gift of prophecy and understand all mysteries, and all knowledge; and have all faith so that I could remove mountain, and

have not love, I am nothing" -1 Corinthians 13:3 KJV

"And now abides faith, hope, love, these three; but the greatest of them is love" -   1 Corinthians 13:13 KJV

The Peace of God in your life is not working because of the absence of the love ingredient in your life. It is sad to say this, but we are getting somewhere that it is becoming difficult to even trust some Christians because the love ingredient is now missing in our generation. This love I am talking about is not somebody giving you flowers. The most difficult part of this love is even loving your enemies. Apostle Paul makes us understand that it is not the one praying in tongues every day that is spiritual, but the one walking in love. We are getting deceived because we are not checking the virtues and the fruits. If you love your wife, you are spiritual; if you submit to your husband, you are spiritual. Love is the fulfillment of the law. If there is anything absent from the church, it is the ingredient of love.

One day the Lord was explaining to me why we easily get divorced. He told me this. Number one; we don't understand covenant and number two; we break all the relationships we establish before we even get married.

The spirit of love is so absent that some of you can develop a relationship for ten years and break it in just one hour, and never come back again. God has a reason for putting the people around you in your life because he doesn't waste His time creating anybody. It may appear as though you don't need them today but you may need them tomorrow. Love is what makes you come back to your husband or your wife and say: "I have walked with you these number of years.

It is not this problem that should separate us". The reason you must do this is that if you are not careful, lack of love can let you forget the investment your partner has made in your life.

What is this love I am talking about?

"Love suffers long, and is kind; love envies not; love vaunts not itself, is not puffed up, does not behave itself rudely, seeks not her own, is not easily provoked, keeps no record of evil; rejoices not in iniquity, but rejoices in truth; bears all things, believes all things, hopes all things, endures all things". - 1 Corinthians 13:4-7

…Refusing to grow

"For when for the time you ought to be teachers, you have need that one teaches you again which be the first oracle of God; and become such as have need of milk and not solid food" - Hebrews 5:12-13

"When I was a child, I spoke as a child, I understood as a child: but when I became a man, I put away childish things" - 1 Corinthians 13:11

"As newborn babes, desire the pure milk of the word, that you may grow thereby" - 1 Peter 2:2

Refusing to grow and staying in your babyhood christianity can affect your 'Peace of God'. I can say this for a fact that most of the troubles we are facing in the church today is because people are not maturing as children of God in their Christian Faith. When you don't act the way you used to act in times past, it is called maturity. Imagine we all come to church and whiles we are seated, everyone is holding a feeding bottle in his or her mouth; think about it, which is exactly the way some people look in the spirit.

There is a place you must graduate from childhood to adulthood. You must not fight people who carry higher authority than you. Don't sit in your room and speak against a man of God, because you are entering into a realm you don't have the grace to handle. Life in the natural comes from the spirit. So, be careful you don't get yourself trapped. If you control your mouth, you control your destiny. That is why people who don't talk much are always wise. They hardly get into trouble. Show me a wife whom when the husband is talking, she is quiet, and I will show you a virtuous woman - You need to grow!

...Refusing to walk in humility

"A man's pride shall bring him low but honor shall uphold the humble in the spirit" -   Proverbs 29:23

"God resists the proud but gives grace to the humble" - James 4:6

"If my people who are called by my name shall humble themselves, and pray, and seek my face, and turn from their wicked ways; then will I hear from heaven, and will forgive their land. -   2 Chronicles 7:14

If you want to establish and maintain the peace of God, walk in humility. The pride in our generation is becoming too much. When you come to a place where you know you have made a mistake, it takes humility to come back, as in the case of the prodigal son (Luke 15:11-32). Humility is what makes you say, "I am sorry" even when you are right. Anybody that struggles to say, "I am sorry" has no future. You will destroy a lot of people God has put around you because of your arrogance. Every relationship will be tested, and when the test comes, it doesn't mean that it calls for separation. "I am sorry for what happened", and the relationship will bounce back strongly. The prodigal son needed to come back in humility, and when he came, the relationship between him and his father bounced back with a celebration.

Humility attracts the mercy of God

Grace is unmerited favor, mercy is unmerited advantage. You deserve to die but mercy says, "No". In the law court, you are supposed to be sentenced but the judge can decide to apply mercy because the law is the bosom of the judge. So, in the judgment seat, God can apply His mercy seat. That is why the Bible says,

"They that will show mercy, I will show mercy (Rom. 9:15).

Let's look at some biblical examples of how humility attracted the mercy of God;

1. 1 Kings 21:20-29

"And Ahab said to Elijah, Have you found me o my enemy? And he answered I have found you: because you have sold yourself to work evil in the sight of the

Lord. Behold, I will bring evil upon you, and will take away your posterity, and will cut off from Ahab every male, and he that is shut up and left in Israel and will make your house like the house of Jeroboam the son of Nebat, and like the house of Baasha the son of Ahijah, for the provocation with which you have provoked me to anger, and made Israel to sin.

And of Jezebel also spoke the Lord, saying, The dogs shall eat Jezebel by the wall of Jezreel. He that dies in the field shall the fowls of the air eat. But there was none like unto Ahab, who did sell himself to work wickedness in the sight of the Lord, whom Jezebel his wife stirred up. And he did very abominably in following idols, according to all things as did the Amorites, whom the Lord cast out before the children of Israel.

And it came to pass when Ahab heard those words, he tore his clothes, and put sackcloth upon his flesh, and fasted, and lay in sackcloth, and went softly. ***And the words of the Lord came to Elijah the Tishbite, saying, see you how Ahab humbles himself before me, I will not bring the evil in his days but in his son's days will I bring the evil upon his house." KJV.***

Which means that, if the son also humbles himself, the Lord will not bring the evil in his days.

2. 2 Chronicles 33:1-13

"Manasseh was twelve years old when he began to reign, and he reigned fifty and five years in Jerusalem but did that which was evil in the sight of the Lord, like unto the abominations of the nations, which the Lord had cast out before the children of Israel. For he built

again the high places which Hezekiah his father had broken down, and he raised up altars for Baalim, and made idol poles, and worshiped all the host of heaven, and served them.

Also, he built altars in the house of the Lord, of which the Lord had said, in Jerusalem shall my name be forever. And he built altars for all the host of heaven in the two courts of the house of the Lord. And he caused his children to pass through the fire in the valley of the son of Hinnom: also he practiced soothsaying, and used witchcraft, and dealt with mediums, and with wizards: he did much evil in the sight of the Lord, to provoke him to anger.

And he set a carved image, the idol which he had made, in the house of God, of which God had said to David and to Solomon his son, In this house, and in Jerusalem, which I have chosen before all the tribes of Israel will I put my name forever. Neither will I any more remove the foot of Israel from out of the land which I have appointed for your fathers; if only they will take heed to do all that I have commanded them, according to the whole law and statutes and ordinances by the hand of Moses. So Manasseh made Judah and the inhabitants of Jerusalem to err and to do worse than the nations, which the Lord had destroyed before the children of Israel.

*And the Lord spoke to Manasseh, and to his people but they would not hearken. Therefore the Lord brought upon the captains of the army of the king of Assyria, who took Manasseh with hooks, and bound him with bronze fetters, and carried him to Babylon. **And when he was in affliction, he sought the Lord his God, and humbled himself greatly before the God of his fathers, and prayed unto him and he received his*** *entreaty, and heard his supplication, and brought him again to Jerusalem into his kingdom. Then Manasseh knew that the Lord was God."KJV*

3. 2 Chronicles 12:5-7

"Then came Shemaiah the prophet to Rehoboam, and to the princes of Judah, that were gathered together to Jerusalem because of Shishak, and said unto them, That says the Lord, You have forsaken me, and therefore have I also left you in the hand of Shishak. The princes of Israel and the king humbled themselves; and said, The Lord is righteous.

And when the Lord saw that they humbled themselves, the word of the Lord came to Shemaiah, saying, They have humbled themselves; therefore I will not destroy them, but I will grant them some deliverance, and my wrath shall not be poured out upon

Jerusalem by the hand of Shishak."KJV

FURTHER READINGS:

LUKE 14:11; PROVERBS 16:5;

PROVERBS 11:2; PROVERBS 29:23

Also By

Nanasei Opoku-Sarkodie

- Breaking Negative Patterns In The Bloodline
- The Atmosphere Of Prayer
- Knowing Who You Are In Christ
- 8 Keys For A New Season
- Divine Health
- Godly Honour
- The Benefits Of Fasting
- The Holy Spirit
- The Just Shall Live By Faith
- Gracious Quotes For Victorious Living
- The Power Of Words
- Fasting 101
- Anger Management-God's Way